Dear Parent:

Congratulations! Your child is taking the first steps on an exciting journey. The destination? Independent reading!

STEP INTO READING® will help your child get there. The program offers five steps to reading success. Each step includes fun stories and colorful art. There are also Step into Reading Sticker Books, Step into Reading Math Readers, Step into Reading Phonics Readers, Step into Reading Write-In Readers, and Step into Reading Phonics Boxed Sets—a complete literacy program with something for every child.

Learning to Read, Step by Step!

Ready to Read   Preschool–Kindergarten
• big type and easy words • rhyme and rhythm • picture clues
For children who know the alphabet and are eager to begin reading.

Reading with Help   Preschool–Grade 1
• basic vocabulary • short sentences • simple stories
For children who recognize familiar words and sound out new words with help.

Reading on Your Own   Grades 1–3
• engaging characters • easy-to-follow plots • popular topics
For children who are ready to read on their own.

Reading Paragraphs   Grades 2–3
• challenging vocabulary • short paragraphs • exciting stories
For newly independent readers who read simple sentences with confidence.

Ready for Chapters   Grades 2–4
• chapters • longer paragraphs • full-color art
For children who want to take the plunge into chapter books but still like colorful pictures.

STEP INTO READING® is designed to give every child a successful reading experience. The grade levels are only guides. Children can progress through the steps at their own speed, developing confidence in their reading, no matter what their grade.

Remember, a lifetime love of reading starts with a single step!

TM and copyright © by Dr. Seuss Enterprises, L.P. 2014.

All rights reserved. Published in the United States by Random House Children's Books, a division of Random House, Inc., New York.

Step into Reading, Random House, and the Random House colophon are registered trademarks of Random House, Inc.

Based in part on *The Cat in the Hat Knows a Lot About That!* TV series (Episode 9) © CITH Productions, Inc. (a subsidiary of Portfolio Entertainment, Inc.), and Red Hat Animation, Ltd. (a subsidiary of Collingwood O'Hare Productions, Ltd.), 2012.

THE CAT IN THE HAT KNOWS A LOT ABOUT THAT! logo and word mark TM 2010 Dr. Seuss Enterprises, L.P., Portfolio Entertainment, Inc., and Collingwood O'Hare Productions, Ltd. All rights reserved. The PBS KIDS logo is a registered trademark of PBS. Both are used with permission. All rights reserved.

Broadcast in Canada by Treehouse™. Treehouse™ is a trademark of the Corus® Entertainment Inc. group of companies. All rights reserved.

Visit us on the Web!
StepIntoReading.com
Seussville.com
pbskids.org/catinthehat
treehousetv.com

Educators and librarians, for a variety of teaching tools, visit us at RHTeachersLibrarians.com

Library of Congress Cataloging-in-Publication Data
Rabe, Tish.
A tale about tails / by Tish Rabe ; based on a television script by Pete Sauder ; illustrated by Tom Brannon. — First edition.
    pages cm. — (Step into reading ; step 3)
Audience: 5–8.
ISBN 978-0-385-37117-9 (trade) — ISBN 978-0-375-97185-3 (lib. bdg.) — ISBN 978-0-375-98172-2 (ebook)
1. Tail—Juvenile literature. I. Sauder, Peter. II. Brannon, Tom, illustrator. III. Title.
QL950.6.R33 2014 591.4′1—dc23 2012047694

Printed in the United States of America
10 9 8 7 6 5 4 3 2 1

A Tale About Tails

by Tish Rabe
based on a television script by Pete Sauder
illustrated by Tom Brannon

Random House 🏠 New York

"You did it!" said Sally.

"Believe it or not,

you taped the tail

in just the right spot!"

"Paper tails are okay," said Nick,

"but how would it feel

if, instead of paper,

we had tails that were real?"

"Tails are great!" cried the Cat.

"Mine helps me beat the heat.

It fans my back.

It makes a great seat.

I use it to jump rope

and turn out the light.

It pulls down the shade

in my bedroom at night."

"I love my tail, too!"

said the Fish with a *splish*.

"I think it's the perfect

tail for a fish."

"It's true," said the Cat.

"His tail helps him swim.

A fish-swishy tail

is the right one for him!"

"A tail," Sally said,

"looks like lots of fun,

but if *I* got a tail,

how would I choose one?"

"I've got it!" the Cat said.

"I know what to do

to find out which tail

is the right one for you!

"To the Thinga-ma-jigger!
And we will set sail
for the faraway Jungle
of Wagga-tag-tail.

"The tails you will see there
you'll never believe,
and once we get there,
you will not want to leave!"

Off to Wagga-tag-tail
they went, and once there
they started looking
for tails everywhere.
"Tails can be short,
curly, fluffy, or long.
First, we'll meet a monkey
whose tail is quite strong."

"Hello!" called the monkey.

"Up here! Look at me!

With my tail, I can swing

branch to branch, tree to tree."

"Your tail," Sally said,

"helps you fly through the air,

but we don't have tails,

so we can't get up there."

"I know," said the Cat,

"how to get tails for you.

I'll call on the help

of Thing One and Thing Two.

You will soon have the best

tails that you've ever seen

when they build you a . . .

". . . Tail-a-ma-fixer machine!
Just step inside it
and soon you will see
you can pick any tail
and the tails are all free."

Nick pushed a button
and said, "Monkey tails, please!
Sally and I want
to swing through the trees."

The Tail-a-ma-fixer
started to quake.
Lights started to flash
and it started to shake.
"Hold on!" Sally said.
And the next thing she knew . . .

. . . she had a tail like a monkey's—
and Nick had one, too!
"With our tails," Sally said,
"we can swing high and low
in the trees like a monkey.
Come on, Cat. Let's go!"

They were starting to swing
in the trees way up high
when they saw a big bird
that came flying on by.
"It's a quetzal," the Cat said,
"and take it from me—
he has one of the prettiest
tails we will see."

"His tail is so bright,"
Sally said to the Cat.
"Can you get us tails
just as pretty as that?"

"We have quetzal tails!" Nick said.

"They're bright blue and green.

They're the prettiest tails

that I've ever seen!"

They flew with the quetzal,
then suddenly heard
a sound that they knew
was not made by a bird.

"Did you hear that?" asked Nick.

"I heard *shake, shake, shake, shake.*"

The Cat said, "That sound's from

the tail of a snake.

That's a rattlesnake,

and its tail makes a sound

to warn everyone

that a snake is around."

"Tails like that could come in
very handy," said Nick.
"I'll push the snake button
and get us some quick!

"Come on, Sally, let's shake
our tails like a snake.
It's easy to do. We just
shake, shake, shake, shake!"

"We've done a tail tour,"
the Cat said, "and have found
some are pretty, some handy,
and some make a sound.
A monkey's tail holds on,
and as you can see,
he needs his strong tail
to live up in a tree.

"A quetzal's tail looks
very pretty and bright.
When he flies through the sky,
it's a beautiful sight.

"A rattlesnake's tail
makes a sound you can hear.
It's this snake's way of warning
that danger is near.

"There are all kinds of tails,
fun, fancy, and fine,
but the tail I like most
in the whole world is . . .

"... mine!"